CW00322464

INVESTIGATION REPORT
OF THE
HOT OIL PIPELINE FAILURE
AT BROMBOROUGH
ON SATURDAY
19th AUGUST 1989

BY

D A SOUTHGATE
PIPELINES INSPECTORATE
SAFETY DIRECTORATE
PETROLEUM ENGINEERING DIVISION
DEPARTMENT OF ENERGY

London: **HMSO**

Preface

At the time of this incident Mr Peter Morrison, then Minister of State for Energy, in a public statement on the matter, said that any lessons from the Department's Investigation which are relevant to other pipeline operators will be circulated immediately to the Industry. A letter drawing attention to the incident and asking pipeline owners to review their operating, inspection and maintenance procedures was sent in October 1989, to all those who might have similar hot oil pipelines. See Appendix "J" to the report.

Finalising the report has taken somewhat longer than anticipated because the investigating inspector required some special work to be carried out by the Corrosion and Protection Centre Industrial Services (CAPCIS), of the University of Manchester Institute of Science and Technology (UMIST) and it was necessary for this work to be completed before final conclusions and recommendations could be drawn.

With the agreement of the Health and Safety Commission, the Department of Energy now wishes the report, which is largely technical in nature, to be made available to the public in its entirety in order to ensure that other operators of similar hot oil pipelines may benefit from the lessons to be learned from the report. However, because of its bulky nature, the CAPCIS report is not included at Appendix "P" as stated in the foreword, but just those figures to which reference is made in the body of the report. The CAPCIS report is available to anyone who wishes to inspect it at the Department of Energy Library, No. 1 Palace Street and in both Libraries of the Houses of Parliament.

CONTENTS

APPENDICES

FOREWORD

TO: THE CHAIRMAN OF THE HEALTH AND SAFETY COMMISSION

On 29th September 1989, pursuant to Section 14(2) (a) of the Health and Safety at Work etc. Act 1974, you authorised me to undertake an investigation into a spillage incident from a pipeline between Tranmere and Stanlow on Merseyside, owned by Shell UK Limited, which took place on Saturday 19th August 1989.

The Terms of Reference were as follows:

> "To establish the facts giving rise to the failure of the pipeline; to ascertain the system of work governing the operation and maintenance of the pipeline at the time of the failure; to consider the health and safety implications of such a system of work and failure; and to make recommendations to the Health and Safety Commission with a view to the avoidance of similar incidents in the future":

and to make a special report thereon.

Pursuant to that authorisation, a full copy of which is included in Appendix A, I now submit my report.

The report contains a description of the pipeline system in which the leak occurred and of the events which took place during and after the incident. It also identifies the cause of the failure and makes specific recommendations regarding the pipeline which failed, as well as making reference to the implications for similar pipelines which are subject to the Pipe-lines Act 1962.

A report from the Consultant engaged to assist in the investigation is attached as Appendix P. This was received in draft in early February and finalised during March.

D A SOUTHGATE
PRINCIPAL PIPELINE ENGINEER
PIPELINES INSPECTORATE
9TH April 1990

1 EXECUTIVE SUMMARY

1.1 At 1500 hours approximately on Saturday 19th August 1989 a 12 inch diameter pipeline carrying hot, Tia Juana Pesado (TJP)—a heavy Venezuelan crude oil—from Tranmere to Stanlow, leaked in the foreshore area of the River Mersey estuary western bank at Bromborough. The pipeline operator, Shell UK Ltd., became aware of a flow discrepancy at about the same time as receiving third-party reports of oil being seen in the foreshore area. The main oil pumps were shut down and pipeline valves were closed at 1526 hours. The leak was located by Shell employees at 1550 hours and work was put in hand immediately to bund off the site which is tidal.

1.2 Because the TJP crude oil would, upon cooling, solidify and block the pipeline, Shell re-started pumping with light oil to displace the crude oil. The light oil was then replaced by water so as to get water to a point downstream of the leak and thus minimise further loss of oil into the river on the next high tide. Concurrently, removal of the crude oil which continued to flow from the leak, was achieved using vacuum pumps discharging into road tankers. At 2000 hours, a dramatic increase in flow from the leak caused Shell to stop the main oil pumps again.

1.3 On Sunday 20th August a temporary clamp was fitted around the leak and pumping of water was resumed. Throughout this period, clean-up operations were undertaken on the river by Shell, the Local Authority and National Rivers Authority officials. Approximately 150 tonnes of oil were lost into the river and about 50 tonnes were recovered into road tankers at the site.

1.4 I proceeded to the site on Monday 21st August to carry out an investigation into the cause of the leak and to assess whether Shell's response was adequate in all the circumstances.

1.5 On Thursday 24th August after the pipeline had been cleared of water, the temporary clamp was removed and I took possession of a two metre length of pipe containing the failure. I instructed the Corrosion and Protection Centre Industrial Services (CAPCIS) of the University of Manchester Institute of Science and Technology (UMIST) to carry out site observations and examine the pipe sample in their laboratories. CAPCIS undertook the work in accordance with a contract with the Department of Energy. CAPCIS had been selected, since the Department suspected that the failure was likely to have been associated with corrosion mechanisms.

1.6 The pipeline generally has a coal tar enamel anti-corrosion coating, covered by thermal insulation which is additionally encased in concrete for stability in the foreshore area. The leak was due to a failure in the pipe wall, as a result of excessive thinning caused by severe localised corrosion, close to a welded butt joint in the pipeline which, it is assumed, had originally been protected by a field joint coating. The corrosion affected an area averaging about 0.5m wide all around the pipe circumference with varying remaining wall thicknesses. Only some 25% of the pipe wall original thickness remained at the point of failure.

1.7 The corrosion was due to the ingress of sea water through the field joint coating, which is considered to have been damaged by thermally-induced differential longitudinal movement between the pipe and its coatings. (In normal operations the pipeline is subject to cyclic temperature variations between ambient and up to 80°C). This phenomenon is described by CAPCIS, which has also advised that the dominant factor is the change in the physical properties of the anti-corrosion coating at 80°C. The pipeline originally operated at 65°C, but additional provisions for pipeline longitudinal expansion were made in 1985 to permit operation at the higher temperature. However no evidence has been found to indicate that adequate consideration was given by Shell to the effect of the higher temperature on the anti-corrosion coating.

1.8 The incident posed no threat to persons at any time but did cause environmental damage as a result of which the National Rivers Authority has successfully prosecuted Shell UK Limited under the Control of Pollution Act 1974.

1.9 As a result of my investigation I concluded that corrosion of the pipeline, as designed and built, was impossible to detect by the cathodic protection system measurements and test observations used by Shell. I also concluded, that a more accurate method of measurement of crude oil transported would have indicated sooner the possibility of a leak and hence have reduced the environmental damage. Furthermore, a repair clamp should have first been applied before line flushing was attempted.

1.10 Immediately following the pipeline repair, Shell carried out modifications to part of the pipeline to enable the running of an internal inspection tool ("intelligent pig") by British Gas On-line Inspection Centre. This survey indicated other similar corrosion sites as well as significant incidence of minor corrosion along the pipeline. These were confirmed by excavation and exposure and remedial action has been put in hand by Shell.

1.11 The pipeline cannot be operated until a Safety Notice has been issued by the Pipeline Inspectorate. This Safety Notice will require Shell to perform a further internal inspection by "intelligent pig" within 6 months. In this way, corrosion will be identified before it becomes structurally significant. The Safety Notice will be valid for only 8 months and will also include other appropriate provisions, pending a review of the inspection data.

1.12 As a result of this incident, a letter has been sent to operators of all similar hot oil pipelines, drawing their attention to this incident and requiring them to determine and be satisfied in respect of the adequacy of their operating, inspection and maintenance procedures as a safeguard against such failures. Operators have also been requested to advise the Department whether these pipelines can accommodate on-line inspection tools.

1.13 It became apparent in the course of my investigation that some operators were not aware of reporting responsibilities for pipeline incidents under the Reporting of Injuries Diseases and Dangerous Occurrences Regulations 1985 (RIDDOR). The opportunity has been taken to remind them of their responsibilities as already noted in the Guidance to RIDDOR.

2 REPORT OUTLINE

2.1 This investigation report concerns an incident which took place on Saturday 19th August 1989. A pipeline operated by Shell UK Limited developed a leak and 150 tonnes of Venezuelan Crude escaped into the River Mersey.

2.2 The incident is described and the cause is identified. Shell's activities at the time are outlined and a conclusion is drawn. Their inspection and maintenance procedures and the associated implications are also discussed. Recommendations are made regarding the future operation of the pipeline in the short-term. Reference is made to aspects which may affect similar onshore pipelines controlled by the Pipe-lines Act 1962.

2.3 A conclusion is drawn regarding the health and safety implications.

3 DESCRIPTION OF THE PIPELINE

3.1 Pipeline Route

3.1.1 The route of the pipeline used for TJP crude oil transfers, together with salient features is shown on Fig. 1, which also shows the location of the pipeline leak on the Bromborough foreshore, at Ordnance Survey reference SJ360832.

3.1.2 A simplified process flow-scheme depicting the flowpath of TJP from Tranmere to Stanlow is given on Fig. 2.

3.1.3 The pipeline nominal diameter is mainly 12 inches and extends for approximately 19 kilometres between Tranmere and Stanlow. In reality, it is in two sections, Tranmere to Eastham and Eastham to Stanlow, with a cross-over at the old Eastham Oil Depot.

3.1.4 The section between Tranmere and Eastham is about 10 kilometres long. The Shell designation is YP2140. The pipeline has a coal tar enamel anti-corrosion coating and is thermally insulated and substantially buried (0.9m nominal depth) apart from the final 1.5 kilometres which is in an open pipe track as far as Eastham Oil Storage Depot. For a distance of 1 kilometre the pipeline is routed along the Bromborough foreshore area where it set in a trench cut in rock and then back-filled. Because this portion is in tidal, esturine waters, the pipeline is also concrete coated to provide negative buoyancy.

3.1.5 In this section YP2140 the 12 inch nominal diameter pipe is of API 5L grade B steel and 0.330 inch pipe wall thickness. Further details of YP2140 are given in Appendix B. A detailed longitudinal section through a typical field joint in the foreshore area of pipeline YP2140 is shown in Appendix P figure 50.

3.1.6 A 16 inch diameter crude oil pipeline, 1 metre away, occupies the same trench along the foreshore.

3.1.7 The section between Eastham Oil Storage Depot and Stanlow Refinery is about 9 kilometres long. The Shell designation is YP1121. It begins with a short 16 inch diameter section which passes underneath the Manchester Ship Canal and continues in a 12 inch diameter pipe above ground along the eastern bank. The above ground portion is thermally insulated and externally metal clad.

3.1.8 Provision for thermal expansion is made in both sections YP2140 and YP1121. Expansion bellows are installed in the Section between Tranmere and Eastham with expansion loops between Eastham and Stanlow. Anchor blocks are installed throughout.

3.1.9 No pipeline pigging facilities existed for either section at the time of the incident. Neither was the pipeline capable of being inspected with "intelligent pigs" due to the radii of the bends originally installed being too small.

3.2 Pipeline Construction Dates

3.2.1 the two principal sections which comprise the Tranmere to Stanlow pipeline were constructed approximately 19 years apart.

3.2.2 The section (YP1121) between Stanlow refinery and Eastham was originally installed for black oils use in 1953, whereas the section (YP2140) between Tranmere and Eastham was commissioned in 1972. The pipeline sections were up-graded to the current operating conditions in 1985.

3.2.3 The cross-over (YP2732), linking the two sections at Eastham, was installed in 1986. This efectively by-passed the Eastham Oil Storage Depot and created a single pipeline system.

3.3 Pipeline Testing

3.3.1 Prior to commissioning the section (YP2140) was hydrostatically tested with water to 73 bar for 24 hours after cycling the pressure twice between 20 bar and 73 bar.

3.3.2 Since 1979 periodic pressure tests (at intervals of no longer than 2 years) have been carried out using the shut-in head of the pumps at Tranmere, ie. approximately 10% in excess of the maximum working pressure. These tests are maintained for a 24 hour period to demonstrate the tightness of the pipeline system. The most recent test was carried out in February 1988.

3.4 Pipeline Operating Conditions

3.4.1 Originally, the YP2140 pipeline was designed for a maximum inlet temperature of 65.6°C and a maximum operating pressure of 48 bar.

3.4.2 In order to handle TJP, the design inlet temperature was raised to 80°C. For this, 5 additional bellows were installed to allow for increased expansion. The maximum working pressure however, was reduced to 40 bar.

3.4.3 Pressure and temperature controllers at Tranmere modulate pipeline pressure and temperature.

3.4.4 Typically, the pipeline operates in the range 35-40 bar and 65-80°C, whilst transporting hot TJP.

3.5 Cathodic Protection System

3.5.1 In the rocky foreshore area, cathodic protection is provided by a total of four 90 kg magnesium alloy anodes buried on the river side of the pipeline route and located approximately 200m apart. These anodes are connected to both the YP2140 pipeline and the parallel 16 inch pipeline by cables. The rest of the YP2140 pipeline is electrically isolated from the foreshore area and an impressed current system is used for cathodic protection.

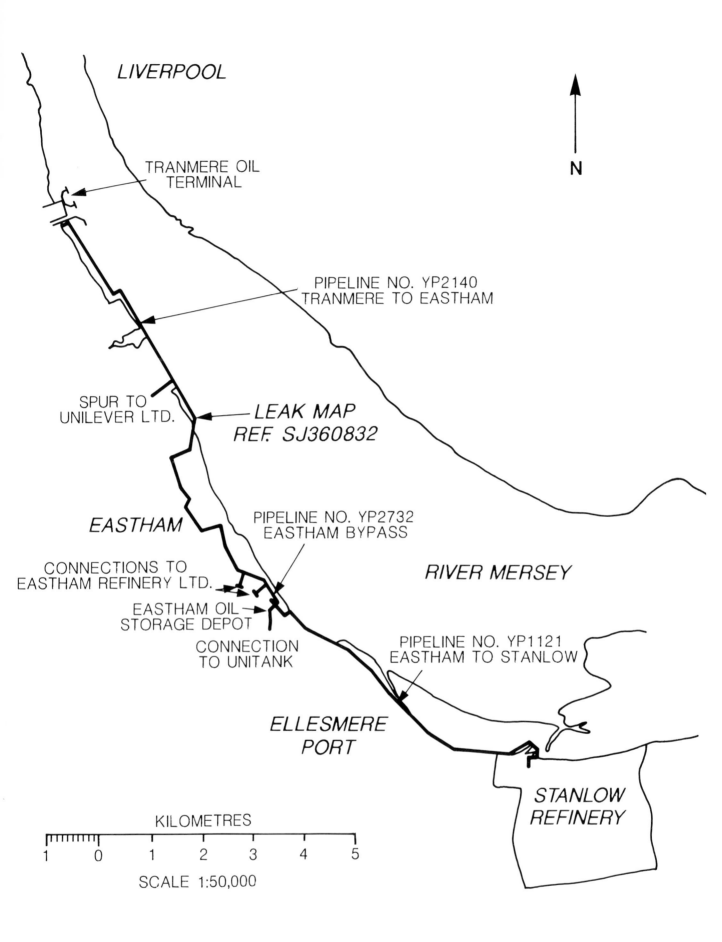

LIVERPOOL

TRANMERE OIL
TERMINAL

N

PIPELINE NO. YP2140
TRANMERE TO EASTHAM

SPUR TO
UNILEVER LTD.

LEAK MAP
REF. SJ360832

EASTHAM

PIPELINE NO. YP2732
EASTHAM BYPASS

CONNECTIONS TO
EASTHAM REFINERY LTD.

RIVER MERSEY

EASTHAM OIL
STORAGE DEPOT

CONNECTION
TO UNITANK

PIPELINE NO. YP1121
EASTHAM TO STANLOW

ELLESMERE
PORT

STANLOW
REFINERY

KILOMETRES

1   0   1   2   3   4   5

SCALE 1:50,000

PIPELINE ROUTE MAP   FIGURE 1

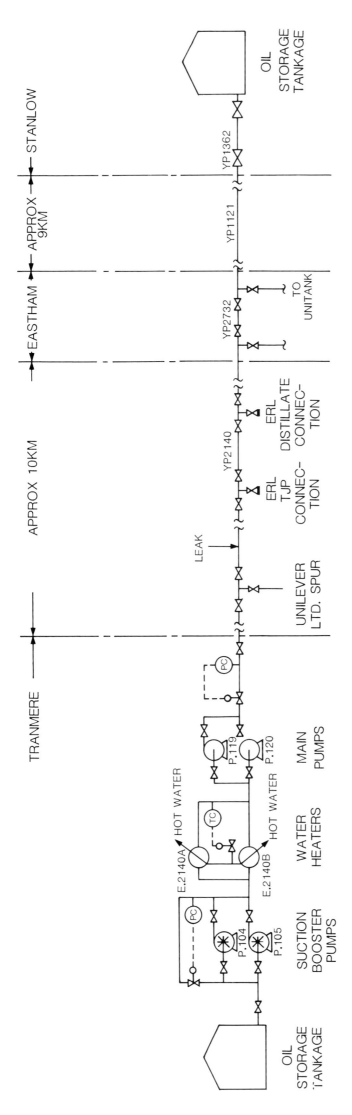

PIPELINE FLOW DIAGRAM

FIGURE 2

4 DESCRIPTION OF THE ASSOCIATED INSTALLATIONS

4.1 General

4.1.1 The relevant schematic of the pipeline and storage facilities at both Tranmere and Stanlow is indicated on Fig. 2, section 3.0.

4.1.2 Tranmere Oil Depot is provided with sea-going tanker discharge facilities including jetties, pipework and oil storage tanks. Dedicated tankage is provided with heaters for black oils use, including TJP.

4.1.3 Suction booster pumps take oil from the storage tanks, passing it through hot water heat exchangers and into the main line pumps. The pipeline flow rate achievable is adjustable between 120 and 600m^3/hour.

4.1.4 A pressure controller (P.C.), in conjunction with a control valve, limits the maximum operating pressure to 40 bar. Should this be exceeded and reach 42 bar an alarm will be given in the Tranmere control room. At 45 bar the main pumps will trip.

4.1.5 The temperature controller controls the heater oil outlet temperature.

4.1.6 At Stanlow similar storage tankage is available.

4.2 Data Logging

4.2.1 Data concerning oil movements within the Tranmere Oil Depot are logged on a computer in the Tranmere control room. In effect, this records the status of various items of equipment, eg. pump "P119 started or stopped".

4.2.2 Pipeline pressure is not recorded. When the P.C. is in "manual mode" only the percentage open position is shown on the computer log. Typically, when the pumps are started the pump discharge valve is completely closed as is the pressure control valve. As the pumps are run up to full speed the pump discharge valve and the pressure control valve are opened progressively until the fully open position is reached. Thereafter, the P.C. modulates the pipeline pressure automatically until a computer logged command initiates a change.

4.2.3 Pipeline Pressure set points are shown on the log during "automatic mode".

4.2.4 Actual pipeline pressure may only be obtained from a locally mounted pressure gauge. The original pipeline pressure recorder in the Tranmere control room was replaced by a computer. Regrettably, therefore, a pressure recorder strip chart is not available. Normally the pressure data history is invaluable for tracing the events surrounding an incident.

4.2.5 A temperature controller controls the heat exchanger oil outlet temperature according to commands entered into the Tranmere control room computer.

4.2.6 Temperature recorder charts are not provided. No temperature cut-outs exist.

4.2.7 A maximum temperature of 80°C is defined in the operating instructions for the YP2140 pipeline leaving Tranmere.

4.3 Tank Dips
4.3.1 The volume of oil transported through the pipeline is measured by comparing the change in tank levels over a given period of time. This procedure is known as "tank dipping".

4.3.2 Remote tank level indicator gauges are situated in the control rooms at both Tranmere and Stanlow. Readings are normally made at hourly intervals.

5 OPERATIONAL ASPECTS

5.1 TJP arrives at Tranmere in heated sea-going tankers and is discharged into storage tanks provided with heating facilities to maintain 60°C. Hot water heaters are used to raise the temperature to 70/80°C upstream of the main pumps (Fig. 2, section 3).

5.2 Of four pipelines available between Tranmere and Stanlow, the YP 2140/YP 1121 pipeline is the only one used for TJP.

5.3 The temperature gradient along the thermally insulated pipeline between Tranmere and Stanlow results in an arrival temperature of about 60°C. Pipeline pre-heating for the introduction of TJP is not required. However, the high viscosity characteristics of TJP necessitate the pipeline being flushed out at the end of each transfer.

5.4 If this were not done, the TJP would cool down to a point where the oil would no longer be pumpable at the pipeline pressures available. Effectively, the pipeline would become totally blocked. A light, low viscosity flushing oil is used to displace the TJP.

5.5 Transfers of TJP between Tranmere and Stanlow are made intermittently and, following flushing, the pipeline is then shut down sometimes for periods of up to two weeks or more.

6 THE INCIDENT

6.1 Events prior to 1500 hours on Saturday 19th August 1989

6.1.1 Prior to the incident on the 19th August the pipeline had been shut down for 15 days and contained a low viscosity flushing oil.

6.1.2 To prepare the pipeline for the crude oil transfer, heated heavy fuel oil was pumped into the pipeline at Stanlow to displace the low viscosity flushing oil into tankage at Tranmere. This was done to ensure that an adequate volume of flushing oil was available at Tranmere in order, eventually, to displace the crude oil from the pipeline to Stanlow. Total pipeline volume is approximately 1,400m^3.

6.1.3 Reference should be made to Figures 1 and 2 in order to follow the sequences given below.

6.1.4 At 0948 hours on 19th August pumps were prepared and valve settings were made in readiness for the crude oil transfer. Both of the suction booster pumps P104/105 were run and then stopped.

6.1.5 At 1024 hours both of the suction booster pumps and the main pump P.119 were put into full operatiuon and initially the pressure controller was manually set to 20% open.

6.1.6 The transfer of crude oil had begun. The batch size was 5,000m^3.

6.1.7 Following the start of the crude oil transfer there were two periods during which the pressure controller was automatically modulating the pipeline pressure. These were between 1045 hours–1055 hours and 1139 hours–1421 hours. The pressure controller was set at 39 and 40 bar respectively. The flowrate was approximately 140m^3/hour.

6.1.8 At 1421 hours the main pump P.119 tripped due to low suction pressure and four attempts were made to re-start the pump, but again it tripped. The fifth attempt was successful and at 1447 hours the crude oil transfer was resumed.

6.2 Events between 1500 hours and 2000 hours on Saturday 19th August 1989

6.2.1 At about 1500 hours an apparent discrepancy was found between the tank dips measured at Tranmere and Stanlow respectively. See Appendix E for a copy of the tank dips recorded from the commencement of the transfer. Whilst this was being checked two reports were received that oil had been seen on the river. One was a telephone call from a ship in the Bromborough area and the Port Radar Station also contacted Tranmere with the same message.

6.2.2 The Shell operators who were checking the tank dips had decided to keep the situation under observation, but after telephone calls were received the crude oil transfer to Stanlow was stopped by the Shift Supervisor.

6.2.3 Timings differ between two shift operators' logs, see Appendix C. The computer log, however, records at 1526 hours "P.119 STOP" and also, but in manuscript, is written "closed main valve".

6.2.4 At 1500 hours one of the operators walking the pipeline route found the

11

leak on the YP2140 section and reported the position back by radio to the Tranmere control room. Called out by the Shift Supervisor, the Duty Officer, together with the Duty Engineer, immediately went to the location on Bromborough foreshore.

6.2.5 At 1559 hours, flushing oil from Tank 6013 at Tranmere was pumped into the pipeline but after a short while the leakage of oil started to increase and the Duty Officer ordered the transfer to be stopped. By 1621 hours the system was shut down and the main block valve at Tranmere closed. The section of pipeline containing the leak was then isolated by closing valves at Eastham and at the branch connection to Unilever on the Tranmere side of the leak.

6.2.6 By 1630 hours additional Refinery staff had been mobilised together with vacuum road tankers fitted with hoses for recovering oil. By this time a bund was being constructed around the location of the leak using stones and sand to form a catchment pool from which the vacuum tankers could recover oil. Based upon previous experience that oil recovery using vacuum tankers and hoses was likely to be a successful operation, Shell decided to pump water into the pipeline at Tranmere in a controlled manner. It was realised that oil would continue to escape from the pipeline but it was thought that it could be recovered without causing further pollution. The purpose was to displace the oil beyond the leakage point. Shell considered that this would minimise further leakage of oil into the river when the tide covered the area. Otherwise, oil escaping due to natural draining down would float away.

6.2.7 At 1936 hours, with the assistance of a crude oil tanker at the jetty at Tranmere, water was pumped into the pipeline. The vacuum tankers stood in readiness to recover any oil which might escape into the bund catchment pool. This operation continued satisfactorily until at 2000 hours the leak increased dramatically to a substantial upward spray. Shell calculated that about 7 tonnes of TJP escaped at this stage. The Tranmere control room computer log shows that pump P.119 was stopped at 1005 hours. The leak point was again isolated with valves being closed at Tranmere, Eastham and at the branch connection to Unilever.

6.3 Events between 2000 hours on Saturday 19th August and 2400 hours on Sunday 20th August 1989

6.3.1 During the late evening, after the section of pipeline containing the leak had been isolated, other sections of the pipeline were flushed out to remove the oil.

6.3.2 Between 2130 hours and 2250 hours the section of the pipeline between Tranmere and Unilever was flushed into Unilever tankage.

6.3.3 At 2315 hours pipeline flushing from Stanlow Refinery to Eastham tankage was commenced. This was completed on Sunday 20th August.

6.3.4 Prior to the high tide in the early hours on 20th August it was found that oil had ceased to leak naturally from the pipeline split: there had been a natural drain down to the low point within the bunded catchment area. The vacuum tankers had continued to recover oil during this time. To gain direct access to the pipeline the concrete capping, about 1.5 m wide and 30 cm thick, first had to be broken up and removed. See Appendix P Fig 5. The pipeline was then fully excavated by hand digging. This enabled the split to be temporarily plugged and covered with dry cement powder. Little further leakage took place during the early morning high tide.

6.3.5 At 1820 hours water was pumped into the pipeline at Tranmere at a low pressure. The vacuum tankers were available and in operation during this time.

6.3.6 At 2040 hours water arrived at the leakage point and a temporary clamp was bolted on to the pipeline, covering the leak point. Water pumping was then resumed at 3.5 bar and the clamp was found to be effective.

6.3.7 The vacuum tankers continued to recover oil from the area of the leak and it is estimated that in all more than 50 tonnes of oil were recovered in this way. The oil was returned to Stanlow Refinery. This quantity was additional to the estimated 150 tonnes which escaped into the river.

6.4 Subsequent Events

6.4.1 Water flushing from Tranmere to Eastham continued until 1104 hours on Wednesday 23rd August.

6.4.2 At 12.45 hours, since no permanent facilities were available, portable air compressors were used at Eastham to displace the water contained in the pipeline back to Tranmere. A separation sphere was not used, however, because Shell was confident that the capacity of the air compressors was adequate.

6.4.3 At 1000 hours on Thursday 24th August, the air compressors were temporarily stopped when it was observed that scant water was exiting from the pipeline at Tranmere. The pipeline valve at Tranmere was then closed. The pipeline was then pressurised with air to 5 bar. It was then blown down at Eastham with the effect of removing further droplets of water.

6.4.4 At 1300 hours the clamp around the pipeline leak point was slackened. This showed intermittent water spray with an oil trace. The vacuum tankers were available but not required.

6.4.5 By 1700 hours the pipeline pressure was virtually down to zero. The clamp was left in position until the imminent high tide had receded. By means of mechanical cutters the pipeline wall was cut halfway through at two selected points, one each side of the leak point. Further cutting had to await the turn of the tide.

6.4.6 High tide was at 1735 hours but it was below the level of sand bags which had been placed to form a bund around the open trench.

6.4.7 At 1745 hours the clamp was unbolted. A 150mm long rupture was found about half way up the pipe on the river side of the pipeline.

6.4.8 At 1800 hours the two pipeline cuts were completed and a 2.3 metre section of pipe containing the rupture was removed. The vacuum tankers were used for a short period to clear a few inches of oily water from the bottom of the trench.

6.4.9 The Department of Energy had already contracted with the Corrosion and Protection Centre Industrial Services (CAPCIS) of the University of

Manchester Institute of Science and Technology (UMIST) to provide specialist support services. The scope of work is given in Appendix N and extracts from the Report issued in March are included in Appendix P.

6.4.10 CAPCIS visited the site on Thursday 24th August and obtained various samples of soil and water effluents which discharge onto the Bromborough foreshore. Cathodic protection test post readings were also taken. Video films and photographs were also taken of the events leading up to and including the removal of the pipe section.

6.4.11 During the morning of Friday 25th August, the section of pipe which had been removed the previous day was generally inspected and photographed. Then, under my control, it was taken to Stanlow Refinery for Shell inspection prior to being transported to the CAPCIS laboratories at UMIST. See Appendix P Fig 10.

6.4.12 At this time no attempt was made to clean the pipe sample taken into my care, in order to preserve any materials adhering to the pipe for examination under laboratory conditions.

6.4.13 Whilst no trace could be found of the original field joint wrapping material, it is assumed that this became dislodged during the excavation and clamping operations and was subsequently lost when oil-contaminated sand was removed from the area.

7 CAUSE OF THE FAILURE

7.1 Failure of the pipeline occurred as a result of external corrosion at the location of the field joint, following the ingress of estuarine water beneath the anti-corrosion coating. Corrosion occurred in a band all the way round the pipe, the width of the band being greatest at the bottom (approximately 55cm) and smallest at the top (approximately 20cm). The band of corrosion was centred approximately 45cm from a cirumferential field weld joint to another pipe section. Outside this severely corroded area, no external corrosion of the pipeline had occurred at this location. There was no internal corrosion.

7.2 External corrosion had occurred to the stage where the remaining wall thickness at the failure point was unable to contain the internal pressure. Bulging of the pipe wall occurred followed by splitting or tearing along the bulge in the axial direction of the pipeline. See Appendix P Fig 14a and 14b.

7.3 The CAPCIS work concluded that the field joint coating had failed as a result of differential movement between the steel pipe, the anti-corrosion and insulation coatings and the outer concrete coating allowing estuarine water to come into contact with the pipe surface. This differential movement is considered by CAPCIS to have been induced by thermal cycling resulting from the intermittent transportation of hot crude oil.

7.4 CAPCIS also concluded that the dominant factor is the change in physical properties of the coal tar enamel coating above 65°C. At these temperatures the coal tar enamel softens and, under longitudinal strain, disbonds from the steel surface. An additional factor is the loss of bond between the polypropylene sheath (around the thermal insulation) and the outer-most coating of concrete. See Appendix P, Fig 49 for a typical pipeline cross-section.

I agree these findings.

15

8 REVIEW OF SHELL'S INSPECTION AND MAINTENANCE PROCEDURES

8.1 Routine inspection and maintenance conducted by Shell of the pipeline and its route prior to the incident comprised:-

(a) Fortnightly observations at road crossings (for potential third-party activities);

(b) Annual walking of the entire route to ensure access;

(c) Six-monthly cathodic protection system measurement surveys;

(d) Pressure testing to 110% of maximum operating pressure at one to two yearly intervals (since 1979);

(e) Inspection and maintenance at each end (above ground sections).

See Appendix M for the pipeline inspection history for YP 2140.

8.2 These activities generally reflect normal oil industry practice. However, CAPCIS has concluded that the cathodic protection surveys performed by Shell would not have been able to detect the particular corrosion processes occurring in this foreshore area, due to the shielding effect of the coatings. Such corrosion is detectable by internal inspection devices ("intelligent pigs") but the pipeline had not been designed to accept them because reliable "intelligent pigs" were not then commercially available, although they have become so since.

8.3 The CAPCIS Report criticised the cathodic protection system as designed and installed in the foreshore area, and commented on the apparent lack of appreciation by Shell of the limitations of their survey techniques and the apparent lack of follow-up by Shell concerning some significant changes in the survey results.

9 REVIEW OF SHELL'S RESPONSE TO THE INCIDENT

9.1 Initial Control Room Response

9.1.1 Exact timings of the third–party reports of oil sightings on the Mersey are not available. Neither can it be assumed that clocks/watches were synchronised. However, the Tranmere control room operator's log states "1510 phone call ex–w/oils ship at Bromborough. Reported oil in river. Trans shut-down". (See Appendix C).

9.1.2 It would appear that the Shift Supervisor (see Appendix D for outline organogram) must have returned at about 1520 to receive the report that oil had been seen in the Mersey, whereupon he shut down the pumps. The computer log shows the shut-down was at 1526 hours. The volume of oil pumped from the Tranmere tank between 1500 and 1526 hours is consistent with the computer log timing.

9.1.3 It would therefore appear that, whilst the Supervisor acted promptly, his control room staff were slow in reacting to the situation.

9.1.4 Examination of the tank dip records (see Appendix E) shows that there was a discrepancy between the volume delivered from Tranmere and the volume received at Stanlow, as measured at 1500 hours. Yet, at 1330 hours, a discrepancy $+231\text{m}^3$ was shown. Reasonable agreement existed at 1400 hours, ie. $+6\text{m}^3$. But, at 1500 hours, a loss of -83m^3 was indicated. When pumping had ceased, an overall loss of 149m^3 was shown. [1m^3 approximately $=1$ tonne].

9.1.5 Although tank dipping is widely used in the oil industry it is not considered to be sufficiently sensitive for indicating the pipeline leakage which in fact occurred. 100m in Stanlow tank 279 represents 186m^3. This volume also approximates to the hourly pumping rate. Oil turbulence within the storage tank and high winds, in particular, can affect tank dip readings. A more reliable method of tank dipping is by manual use of a steel tape and reference to tank calibration tables. This, of course, can only be carried out satisfactorily when oil movements cease and is therefore not appropriate as a means of leak detection for operational purposes.

9.1.6 It would seem, therefore, in the light of this evidence, that the Shell operators' decision to continue to monitor the situation by tank dipping was reasonable. The reports of oil in the river became the over–riding factor which led to the shut-down.

9.2 Subsequent Actions Taken

9.2.1 Shell procedures make clear reference to the requirement for TJP crude oil to be cleared from the line at the end of any transfer, by the use of light flushing oil. Shell's reason for this is that the pipeline would cool down to the point where the TJP crude oil would become unpumpable and thus block the pipeline. See Appendix F for viscosity data. However, there appears to be no relevant instruction for emergency situations such as leaks. The use of light flushing oil at this stage is questionable. There should have been some awareness of the allowable shut-down period following which the re-start of pumping could be ensured.

9.2.2 The Shift Supervisor acted promptly in calling out the Duty Officer and notifying the coastguard at 1530. Shell's Duty Officer acted correctly soon after 1559 hours, when he ordered the flushing operation to cease on noticing an increase in the leak rate.

9.2.3 Shell were then concerned that oil was continuing to drain down to the leakage point and that the next high tide would flood the site, and cause further pollution in the river. They therefore resumed flushing with sea-water at 1936 hours in the hope of displacing the oil past the leak point before the next high tide.

9.2.4 The leak obviously got worse only half an hour after sea-water flushing had commenced. The resulting spray overtopped the bund, thereby causing more oil to escape into the river.

9.2.5 Although Shell believed their actions to displace the TJP were appropriate, in the event it was possible some 24 hours later to clear the pipeline without any particular difficulties. Furthermore, alternatives to displacing the TJP past the leak point, such as increasing the dimensions of the bund and providing additional vacuum tankers, could have been considered. It would seem, therefore, that the initial decision to pump flushing oil was taken prematurely and the correctness of the later decision to pump water is questionable.

9.3 Preparedness for Emergencies

9.3.1 A temporary repair clamp to stop or reduce leakage was not affixed to the pipeline until late evening on Sunday 20th August. This clamp was fabricated by Shell at Stanlow, since no stock of repair clamps was held by Shell. These are however readily available from commercial sources and many operators hold stocks of such equipment.

9.3.2 The Pipeline Emergency Manual gives adequate points of contact and procedures for receipt of incoming third party reports and for call out of Shell staff in an emergency. However, it lists only very basic equipment for emergency use and none for a leak of the type which occurred.

9.3.3 I submit that the Pipeline Emergency Manual did not adequately address the action to be taken in the event of a leak. It should have made reference to the need for repair clamps to be available immediately. Had it done so, Shell would have been able to attach a clamp soon after the leak was identified, thereby reducing leakage significantly.

9.3.4 The Manual makes no reference to any advice with regard to permissible periods of shut-down when the pipeline contains TJP crude oil.

9.3.5 Shell maintained that due to the presence of the concrete capping (see Appendix P Fig 5) and because the pipeline was buried, the clamp could not be installed immediately. Operations were said to have been delayed by the necessity to wait for low tides in order to commence excavation of the pipeline. This was completed and the clamp installed during the second low tide on 20th August. Nevertheless, I consider that Shell should have commenced preparations for installing a clamp sooner than 20th August. This could have been achieved if suitable equipment for removing the concrete capping had quickly been made available.

10 OTHER MATTERS RELEVANT TO THE INVESTIGATION

10.1 Subsequent Internal Inspection

10.1.1 On 12th September, after modifications to the YP2140 section (eg. the installation of long radius bends), an internal inspection of YP2140 using an "intelligent pig" was completed by British Gas, who were working under contract to Shell.

10.1.2 This inspection revealed a total of 13 other locations on YP2104 having significant metal-loss features. Whilst three of these were in the foreshore area, ten others were located elsewhere along the pipeline. (See Appendix G.)

10.1.3 A large number of less serious corrosion features were also disclosed by the inspection. Notable was the corrosion that had occurred in the above-ground section of YP2140. Here, the lagging beneath the metal cladding had become saturated with water and due to the coal tar enamel deterioration by high temperature, conditions favourable to corrosion had thus been established. (See Appendix H).

10.1.4 The YP1121 pipeline, has not been inspected and therefore detailed information on its condition is not available. However, since a large part of YP1121 is above ground and lagged with similar materials to the above-ground portion of the YP2140 pipeline, there is good reason to suppose that significant corrosion will have taken place. The YP1121 line is also 19 years older than YP2140.

10.2 Additional Work by CAPCIS

10.2.1 The Department of Energy contract with CAPCIS was extended to include the examination of a sample of nine further locations along YP2140, including those excavations which were made to check the features indicated by the British Gas "intelligent pig" (see Appendix I). These examinations provided confirmation of the failure mechanism proposed by CAPCIS and also demonstrated the poor arrangements for cathodic protection in the foreshore.

10.3 Future Operation of the Pipeline

10.3.1 The CAPCIS report confirms that a resumption of operation of YP2140 involving thermal cycling will lead to differential movement, damage to the pipeline coating, corrosion and risk of failure of the pipeline.

10.3.2 CAPCIS also undertook tests which confirmed that the coal tar enamel had deteriorated significantly as a result of high temperatures driving out the volatile constituents from the material. The resulting brittle nature of the coal tar enamel at ambient temperatures therefore rendered it susceptible to cracking and disbondment with the attendant loss of performance as an anti-corrosion coating.

10.3.3 In view of the foregoing, there must be doubts whether the YP2140 pipeline will prove economic to maintain in the longer term. Shell will presumably consider at some stage whether the pipeline should be replaced, but in the meantime, they will have to monitor closely the continued integrity of the pipeline and satisfy the Pipelines Inspectorate in this respect.

10.3.4 However, a short-term operation of the YP2140 pipeline can be considered as reasonable, providing the following matters are properly addressed by Shell before the pipeline is brought into use:-

(a) appropriate corrective action at all significant corrosion sites;

(b) a successful hydrostatic pressure test to 1.5 times the maximum operating pressure;

(c) adequate and appropriate emergency procedures;

(d) enhancement of the pipeline supervisory and control systems and route surveillance procedures;

(e) evidence of satisfactory welds on all replacement sections of the pipeline.

10.3.5 Additionally, it will be necessary to repeat the internal inspection with the "intelligent pig" after 6 months in order to monitor the growth rates of defects and also to fit an effective leak detection system.

10.3.6 With the foregoing provisos, I believe that an Operational Safety Notice, having a limited validity of 8 months, can be issued to Shell with minimal risk of a further leak within that timescale and I therefore recommend that course of action. The pipeline cannot be used until this Safety Notice has been issued.

10.3.7 The corrective action for the YP2140 pipeline includes cutting out all the significant corrosion sites, which will ensure that no corrosion sites having a depth in excess of 30% of pipeline wall thickness will remain. However, there will be several residual corrosion sites with a depth of up to 30% of wall thickness. The pipeline also has a minimum wall thickness (due to manufacturing tolerances) of 87.5% of the nominal thickness. Taking the pessimistic assumption that the residual corrosion sites and the areas of minimum wall thickness may coincide, the remaining wall thicknesses will be at least 5.13mm.

10.3.8 For 40 bar operation the required wall thickness in 3.77mm. Thus there is an allowance for further corrosion of at least 1.36mm.

10.3.9 Laboratory measurements by CAPCIS indicate that the parent metal wall thickness adjacent to the corroded area at the failure location averaged 8.35mm. The residual wall thickness at the point of failure was 2mm, and therefore the wastage through corrosion was 6.35mm. Assuming (pessimistically) that all the corrosion occurred between January 1985 and August 1989, the wastage rate then averaged 1.4mm per annum. It should be noted that this occurred in the extremely aggressive environment of the Bromborough foreshore, where intermittent wetting by sea-water took place. Corrosion rates elsewhere are very unlikely to approach 1.4mm per annum and therefore the 1.36mm allowance should be more than sufficient.

10.3.10 This approach is very conservative in that, where localised corrosion exists, normally credit is given for the supporting strength of the surrounding metal. This beneficial factor has been ignored.

10.3.11 Based upon this conservative approach, I confidently conclude that it would be safe for the pipeline to be returned to use, after a hydrostatic pressure test, provided that the "intelligent pig" pipeline inspection is repeated within 6 months of operation. In this way, the progress of corrosion can be tracked and corrective action taken in good time.

10.3.12 On account of the embrittled condition of the coal tar enamel, repeated hydrostatic pressure testing to high levels is not considered to be the best method for pipeline revalidation.

10.3.13 The situation should be further reviewed in the light of an assessment of the additional internal inspection results, before a further Safety Notice can be contemplated.

10.3.14 So far as the YP1121 pipeline is concerned, since no detailed information is available on its condition, a resumption of its operation cannot be contemplated. Shell have not requested that YP1121 be brought back into use, since it is understood that they plan to use TJP at Eastham in future, rather than at Stanlow.

10.4 Other Hot Oil Pipelines
10.4.1 As a result of this incident, a letter has been sent to all pipeline operators having similar hot oil pipelines, drawing their attention to the incident and requiring them to determine and to be satisfied with the adequacy of their operating, inspection and maintenance procedures as a safeguard against such failures (see Appendix J).

10.4.2 Operators have also been requested to advise the Department whether their pipelines can accommodate on-line inspection tools.

10.5 Incident Reporting
10.5.1 Shell did not contact the Pipelines Inspectorate or the local Health and Safety Executive office to inform either of this incident. I first contacted Shell at Stanlow on the morning of Monday 21st August and it became apparent that the local Shell personnel were not aware of their responsibilities under the Reporting of Incidents, Diseases and Dangerous Occurrences Regulations 1985 (RIDDOR).

Shell formally reported the incident by telex on 30th August (see Appendix K).

10.5.2 The opportunity has since been taken to remind all pipeline operators of their responsibilities as laid down in the Guidance to RIDDOR (see Appendix L).

11 HEALTH AND SAFETY ASPECTS

11.1 Substances Conveyed by the Pipeline

11.1.1 Typically, TJP has been pumped through the pipeline for about 1.5 days every fortnight. The pipeline therefore has contained TJP under high pressure for about 10% of the time.

11.1.2 The TJP must be displaced by a flushing oil after each transfer and this operation has typically taken about half a day. When stocks of flushing oil get low at Tranmere, the flushing oil itself has been displaced by heavy fuel oil and this operation too has taken about half a day. Thus, in total the pipeline has contained flushing oil at high pressure for up to one day every fortnight, or about 5% of the time.

11.1.3 The pipeline has also transported heavy fuel oil and oil residues at high pressure for about 25% of the time.

11.1.4 When substances are not being pumped, the flushing oil lies in the pipeline at ambient pressures. Typically, this has been the situation for about 60% of the time.

11.2 Properties of the Substances and Risks to Persons

11.2.1 TJP is a heavy crude with a relatively high (closed cup) flash point of 70°C and an auto-ignition temperature above 200°C. It is therefore difficult to ignite, either locally where it may collect as a pool, or remotely where it may disperse across the water.

TJP is also a "dead" crude, having a virtually zero vapour pressure and is therefore free of any gaseous constituents. There is therefore no risk of either remote atmospheric ignition or of inhalation of harmful vapours.

There is of course a risk of scalding, if a person were sprayed by the escaping hot (approximately 60°C to 70°C) TJP. However, this risk is assessed as low in the relatively unpopulated area along the pipeline route. Furthermore, the TJP is conveyed under pressure for only some 10% of the time. Overall, therefore, I believe that the risks to persons from an escape of TJP from the pipeline are very small.

11.2.2 Like TJP, the flushing oil has a relatively high flash point (in the range 65°C to 100°C) and very low vapour pressure and therefore similar considerations apply regarding ignition and inhalation. Since it is introduced into the pipeline at much lower temperatures than TJP, there will be no risk from scalding in the event of an escape. For a large part of the time, it lies in the pipeline at ambient pressure and any leakage would take the form of seepage up through the ground (from the buried sections of the pipeline) or through the lagging (from the above-ground section). Any spillage would be very localised and accordingly risks to persons are judged as minimal.

11.2.3 The heavy fuel oils and oil residues also have relatively high flash points (in the range 65°C to 120°C and 80°C to 150°C respectively) and very low vapour pressures. They are introduced into the pipeline at about 50°C, which is not a sufficient temperature to have the potential for scalding. They also occupy the pipeline for only some 25% of the time. Risks to persons from these substances are again therefore assessed as minimal.

11.2.4 I conclude from the foregoing that a leak of any of these substances from the pipeline would have created very little risk to persons.

12 POLLUTION

12.1 Whilst significant pollution resulted from the incident, this report does not set out to describe or assess the implications involved. Approximately 150 tonnes of heavy Venezuelan Crude Oil were spilled onto the Bromborough foreshore, Wirral and into the Mersey.

12.2 The National Rivers Authority (NRA) decided to prosecute Shell under the Control of Pollution Act 1974. The NRA case was heard in the Liverpool Crown Court on 22nd February 1990, following referral by the local Magistrates Court as the result of a hearing on 6th November 1989. Shell was fined £1 million and ordered to pay costs. They also incurred the clean-up costs on the River Mersey which were reported to amount to £1.4 million.

13 CONCLUSIONS

13.1 The failure of the pipeline was caused by external corrosion leading to thinning of the pipe to the stage where it was unable to contain the internal pressure. Bulging of the pipe-wall, followed by splitting or tearing along the bulge in the axial direction then occurred leading to leakage of the pipeline contents.

13.2 The corrosion occurred as a result of damage to a field joint coating, which allowed the ingress of tidal water. The damage was caused by thermally-induced longitudinal movements of the pipe and its coatings, due principally to loss of adhesion of the coal tar enamel at 80°C.

13.3 Apparently, Shell gave no consideration to the suitability of the coal tar enamel anti-corrosion coating when the maximum pipeline operating temperature was raised to 80°C in 1985.

13.4 The method and frequency of monitoring fluid transfers between tanks at Tranmere and Stanlow was inadequate for detecting the leak which occurred.

13.5 Although pressure and temperature control was apparently satisfactory, there was no monitoring and recording of pipeline pressure and temperature.

13.6 Shell's Emergency Procedures Manual failed to give any instructions on the remedial actions to be taken in the event of a pipeline leak.

13.7 Shell's emergency pipeline repair equipment was not adequate and not readily available.

13.8 There was no guidance, in either Shell's operating instructions or emergency procedures, regarding permissible lengths of time for which the pipeline could be shut-down whilst containing TJP.

13.9 Shell placed the emphasis on displacing the oil past the leak point with water, rather than on sealing off the leak.

13.10 Three consecutive six-monthly cathodic protection system surveys had indicated test points defects and other readings showing significant change, yet apparently no remedial action was taken. (However, it should be noted that these discrepancies did not directly cause the pipeline failure which occurred).

13.11 Because of the nature of the substances conveyed by the pipeline and its intermittent usage, the hazards to persons caused by an escape from the pipeline are considered to be minor.

13.12 Local Shell personnel were not aware of their responsibilities under RIDDOR.

14 RECOMMENDATIONS

14.1 I recommend that Shell UK Limited be given permission to return to use the YP 2140 pipeline between Tranmere and Eastham for a period of 8 months provided that certain matters are satisfactorily completed beforehand and others are implemented at a later stage.

14.2 Those items which need to be completed before the pipeline is returned to service include:-

(a) The replacement of all pipe sections having corrosion sites with a depth more than 30% through the pipe-wall;

(b) The completion of a satisfactory hydrostatic pressure test;

(c) The provision of comprehensive emergency procedures including the availability of emergency equipment and materials;

(d) The incorporation of pipeline pressure, temperature and flow recording equipment at the Tranmere Control Room, together with tank-dip calibration procedures;

(e) The provision of adequate pipeline route surveillance procedures;

(f) A satisfactory result from an audit of all radiographs and welding/welder documentation associated with all replacement sections incorporated into the pipeline.

14.3 The pipeline should be internally inspected by an "intelligent pig" after six months and the results of that inspection assessed before operation for a further period is permitted.

If further operation is then contemplated, Shell should have finalised their proposals for the installation of a mass-balance leak detection system.

14.4 For longer-term use, Shell must address the need for an improved anti-corrosion coating material for the Bromborough foreshore and possibly also elsewhere.

14.5 For similar hot oil pipelines, consideration should be given to re-validation on a periodic basis.

APPENDIX A
AUTHORISATION FROM
CHAIRMAN OF H.S.C.

Health & Safety Commission

Baynards House
1 Chepstow Place
Westbourne Grove
London W2 4TF

Telephone 01-243 6000

Direct Dialling 01-243 6

Fax 01-727 1202

Telex 25683

From the Chairman

Mr D A Southgate
Inspector of Pipelines
Directorate of Safety
Department of Energy
1 Palace Street
LONDON SW1E 5HE

29 September 1989

Dear Mr Southgate

I attach a formal authorisation for you to conduct an
investigation under Section 14(2)(a) of the Health and Safety at
Work etc. Act. No doubt you will ensure that a copy of your
report to the Commission Is placed also in the hands of the
Permanent Secretary at the Department of Energy.

I would be grateful if you would regard that part of your terms of
reference that deals with health and safety implications as
extending to an opinion on your part as to the range of possible
physical consequences that could have flowed from this rupture, or
other breaches of containment in pipes covered by the systems of
work in force.

Yours sincerely

E J CULLEN FEng PhD
Chairman
Enc.

30

Health & Safety Commission

Baynards House
1 Chepstow Place
Westbourne Grove
London W2 4TF

Telephone 01-243 6000

Direct Dialling 01-243 6

Fax 01-727 1202

Telex 25683

THE HEALTH AND SAFETY AT WORK, ETC ACT 1974 (c.37)

The Health and Safety Commission, considering it necessary or expedient to investigate for the general purposes of Part 1 of the Health and Safety at Work etc. Act 1974 the failure on 19th August 1989 at or near Bromborough, Cheshire, of the Tranmere to Stanlow pipeline, resulting in the spillage of crude oil therefrom, hereby authorises, pursuant to section 14(2)(a) of the said Act, with effect from the said 19th August 1989, Donald Alan Southgate, an Inspector of Pipelines in the Directorate of Safety in the Department of Energy, to conduct an investigation into such failure with the following terms of reference, namely:

> **to establish the facts giving rise to the failure of the
> pipeline; to ascertain the system of work governing the
> operation and maintenance of the pipeline at the time
> of the failure; to consider the health and safety
> implications of such system of work and failure; and to
> make recommendations to the Health and Safety Commission
> with a view to the avoidance of similar incidents in the
> future**

and to make a special report thereon.

Dated ....1989.

(Signed) ....
Chairman
Health & Safety Commission.

31

APPENDIX B
PIPELINE DESIGN DETAILS

APPENDIX B
PIPELINE DESIGN DETAILS

APPENDIX B

1. Design Conditions:

Original: Design Temperature 65.6°C

                                   Max. Working Pressure 48 barg

Current (May 1985):   Design Temperature 80°C

                                   Design Pressure 40 barg

The line is installed with class 300 flanges.

2. Design Codes:

Piping Code of Practice: IP Model Code of Safe Practice for Petroleum

                         Pipelines Part 6 1967

                         BS Code of Practice CP 2010 Part 1 1966

Pipe Coating: BS 4164 1967

Welding and Radiograph: API Standard 1104 and BS2600 1962

3. Materials of Construction:

Piping: 12" Nb Sch. 30 seamless pipe to API 5L Gr B.
                         Pipe wall thickness 0.330 inches.

Valves: Class 300 flanged ANSI, full-bore ball
                         valves.

Bellows: 12" Nb axial compensation bellows - butt
                         welded construction. Convolutions in Incoloy
                         825 material of 3 - ply construction, with
                         inner sleeve to Incoloy 825.

                         Maximum axial movement +/- 2 $^{3}/_{8}$". Bellows
                         are provided with a $^{1}/_{8}$" mild steel shroud.

Thermal Insulation: Two inch thick polyurethane foam (PUF)
                         within a polypropylene outer sheath.

34

APPENDIX B

Concrete Coating: Along the Bromborough Foreshore the pipeline has a two inch thick concrete coating at a density of 140 lb/ft.^{3}.

Field Joint: In-situ wrapping with Servicide P500 tape.

Cathodic Protection: The on-shore sections of the pipeline are protected by an impressed current.

The length of line across the Bromborough Foreshore is protected by sacrificial anodes. Test Points are also installed at regular intervals.

Insulating flanges are installed at each end of the rocky foreshore area.

35

APPENDIX C
SHIFT OPERATORS' LOGS

Spillage Log

09.50   Completed L/c from T279 (Stanlow) to T6012

10.30   Commenced L/c from T6013 (T/mere) to T279 (S/

15.30   Received report from R&D panelman of report of
         oil in R.Mersey, Similar report received from
                                      Port Radar
         Shut down transfer osc T6013, 2 operators to check
         & covers.

         Duty Officer informed. Coastguard informed.
              YP2140 isolated at levers spur.
         ~~No2~~ ;Drupa ~~cleared~~ booms with 100m³ Water
         No2 Boom removed from Drupa a No.3 connected.
         to facilitate water wash of YP2140.

                                              Peter Williams

<u>SPILLAGE LOG.</u>

1525   Drupa exported To Tranmere of
        sighting a large oil slick on River.

1935   Drupa com waterwashing 4P2140 to Stanlo

2005   Requested Drupa to stop waterwash. leaka
        too severe.

2130   Arranged with Levers to clear 4P2140
        to their tankage

2140   Arranged with unitank to clear 4P1121
        to their tankage.

2150   Drupa Com waterwashing 4P2140 to Levers

2250   Drupa fin waterwashing 4P2140 to Lever
        370 m³ pumped — line capacity 364 m³

23.5   No 9 Pumphouse com clearing × 4086 - 4P112
        → Unitank.

0305   No9 Pumphouse completed 4C × 4086 - 74P112
        to Eastham - line Quantity = 690 m³
        813 m³ of cutter pumped

                              Norman Guthrie

0950 FIN L/C T279 TO T6012.

1030 COMM L/C T6013 TO TK 279
ONLY ABLE TO GET P104 & P119 ON LINE
RE LINE PRESS 37 BARS.

1450 P119 TRIPPED

RESTARTED PUMP 119 WITH P104 & P105
PRESS ON LINE NOW 32 BARS.

INFORMED WHITE OILS OF REDUCTION IN PRESS,
ASSUMED THAT LINE HAD CLEARED OF ANY
STICKY MATERIAL

1500 RATE FROM T6013 184 M3/P/H
" TO T279 45 M3/P/H.
DISCUSSED DIFERENCE WITH W/O PANEL
T279 DIP RANGING. DECIDED TO KEEP EYE
ON DIPS

1510 PHONE CALL EX W/OILS, SHIP AT BROMBOROUGH
                 REPORTED
DOCK OIL IN RIVER,
        ^
TRANS SHUT DOWN

D. FOSTER & D. BEARDSMORE OUT TO INVESTIGATE
CHECKED AT BROM DOCK & LEVERS CAGE
OIL COMING FROM EASTHAM DIRECTION.

D. BEARDSMORE CONTINUED ON FOOT ALONG
SHORE, D. FOSTER BACK TO MEANWHILE

D.B. REPORTED LEAK AT BACK OF A.S JONSES
YARD

COMM L/C T6012 TO CLEAR T J P FROM LINE
SHUT DOWN RE D.B. REPORTED LEAK TOO BAD.

DRUPA Nº 2 BOOM OFF Nº 3 BOOM ON.
           FOR WATER WASHING LINE.

1830 LINE ISOLATED AT LEVERS SPUR

APPENDIX D
OUTLINE ORGANOGRAM FOR
STANLOW REFINERY

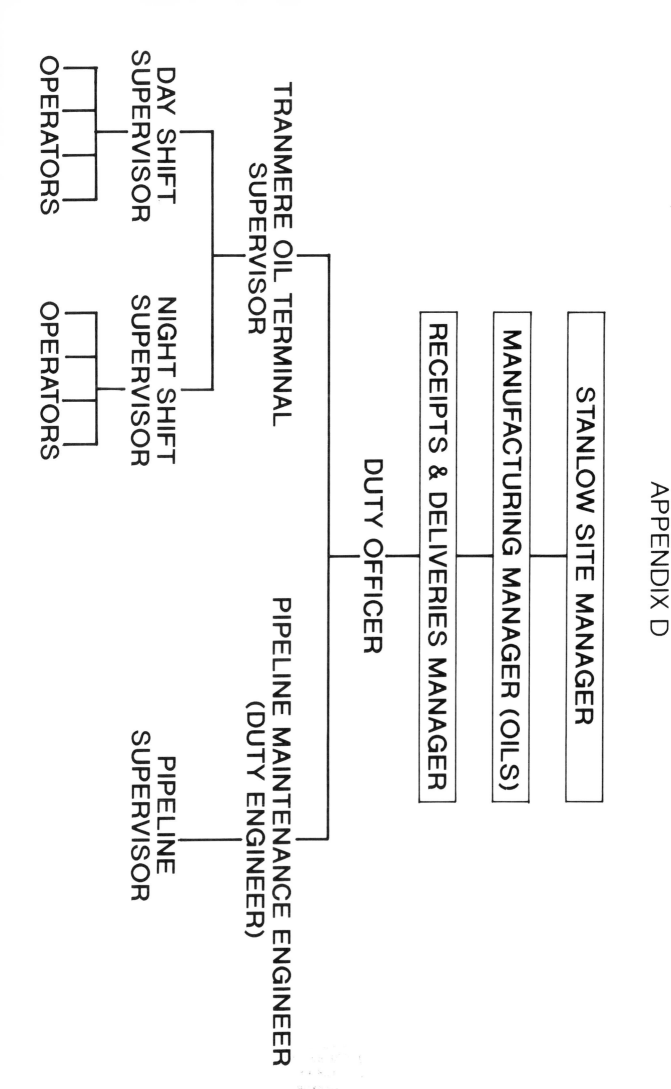

OUTLINE ORGANOGRAM FOR STANLOW REFINERY

APPENDIX D

APPENDIX E
TANK DIP RECORDS

TRANMERE TO STANLOW TRANSFERS   19.8.1989

FROM T 6013   TO T 279 L/C   .07 × 9

M3/M 1865   M3/M 1855

TRANMERE   STANLOW

TIME	DIP	TOTAL TRANS.	TRANS RATE	DIP	TOTAL RECD.	RECD. RATE	TOTAL DIFF.	DIFF LAST HOUR
10.30	4.197			5.153				
1100	4.160	65		5.192	72	72	+ 7	
1130	4.123	135	146	5.226	135	63	+3	
1145	4.107	167	116	5.244	168	135	+ 1	+1
1200	4.088	203	145	5.262	202	136	+1	
1215	4.068	241	150	5.280	236		− 5	
1230	4.050	275	133	5.341	350		+75	
1300	4.015	339	128	5.339	345		+ 6	
1330	3.974	416	154	5.502	647		+231	
1400	3.930	492	152	5.422	493		+ 6	
1500	3.834	676	184	5.473	593	729	−83	
	3.752	829		5.520		650		
						149		

TANK DIPS TABLE

APPENDIX F   OIL PROPERTIES

Oil Properties

Typical data relating to the oils handled in the pipeline at the time of the Incident, are as follows:-

	TJP	Flushing Oil	Heavy Fuel Oil
s.g. @ 15°C	0.9866	0.9624	1.007
Pour Point $^{\circ}$C	+6	0	+9
Viscosity c.s.			
@ 100°C	87.74	11.92	49.7
@ 40°C	3660	108.90	-
@ 20°C	-	359.60	-

APPENDIX G
PRINCIPAL PIPELINE DEFECTS
(IDENTIFIED BY INTERNAL
INSPECTION)

British Gas

On Line Inspection Centre

9.   SUMMARY OF REPORTED FEATURES

| FEATURE NUMBER | EXTERNAL OR INTERNAL | FEATURE DIMENSIONS | | | |
| | | AXIAL (mm) | CIRCUMFERENTIAL (mm) | DEPTH as % of WT | |
				AVERAGE	PEAK
01/1	Ext	50	90	10	29
01/2	Ext	50	250	10	21
02/1	Int	30	29	17	35
03/1	Int	37	37	16	34
04/1	Int	20	26	15	30
05/1	Ext	328	287	8	30
06/1	Ext	400	420	12	35
07/1	Ext	120	190	10	35
08/1	Ext	200	95	12	30
08/2	Ext	45	327	7	15
09/1	Ext	370	130	12	45
10/1	Ext	45	118	20	40
11/1	Ext	40	67	19	40
12/1	Ext	45	72	21	40
13/1	Ext	23	49	17	38

N.B.   FEATURE LOCATIONS ARE GIVEN ON FIG. 7

PRINCPLE PIPELINE DEFECTS SUMMARY SHEET

48

APPENDIX H
PIPELINE DEFECT HISTOGRAM
(SUMMARISING RESULTS OF
INTERNAL INSPECTION)

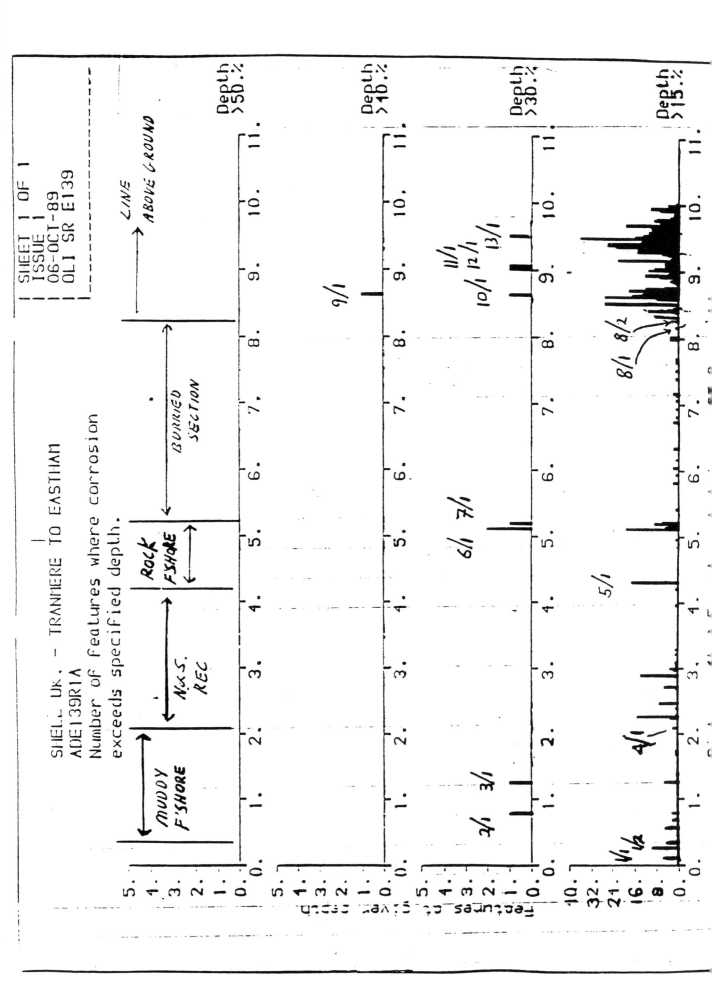

PIPELINE DEFECT HISTOGRAM

APPENDIX I
SKETCH OF FORESHORE AREA

Sketch showing locations of excavations, i.e. failure, CP 0503 and Holes 1 - 7.

APPENDIX J
LETTER TO OPERATORS REF.
INSULATED PIPELINES

Department of Energy

1 Palace Street
London SW1E 5HE

Fax No.	01 834 3771
Switchboard	01 238 3000
Direct Line	01 238

Shell UK Limited
Victoria House
Grosvenor Street
Mold
Flintshire
CH7 1DL

Contact Mr R J Lucas
Tel. ~~01 238 3635~~

Our ref PEP 75/93/20

11th October 1989

For the attention of the Operations Manager

Dear Sir,

1962 PIPE-LINE ACT - OPERATING PIPELINES
EVALUATION AND SURVEY OF INSULATED PIPELINES

Following the oil spill incident at Merseyside in August caused by the rupture of an insulated oil pipeline in a tidal estuary, we consider it essential that operators review their methods of operation and inspection of similar pipelines. You should make an evaluation of your insulated pipelines to determine the adequacy of the operation, maintenance and inspection methods currently being used to ensure their continued integrity and whether any modifications or improvements are required so that you may be satisfied that the likely risk and consequences to the public or environment of a pipeline failure are negligible.

To ensure that our records are satisfactory for insulated pipelines please complete the attached data sheet for each 1962 Act insulated pipeline under your control. The form should be completed as fully as possible and if there are any particular queries please do not hesitate to call us. Such queries should be directed to Mr R Lucas on the above telephone number.

Would you please give this task a high priority and return the data sheet to us by the end of October.

Yours faithfully,
for PIPELINES INSPECTORATE

D R CLEMENTSON
HEAD OF PIPELINES INSPECTORATE

54

APPENDIX K
TELEX REPORT FROM SHELL
(30th AUGUST 1989)

COPY TO Mʳ STEPHENS

✵
  18777 energy g
919651 SHEL O G
ZCZC LTG166 310822 OCV375 310820 RPT OF STW616 STW616 REPEAT OF
ZZ TLEX

FROM SUKL REFINERY STANLOW OMR/11/20 ++ J. FEGAN TLX 629304
URGENT URGENT TO PIPELINE INSPECTORATE (DEPT OF ENERGY) LONDON
ATTN MR CLEMENTSON MR SOUTHGATE
TELEX G 918777 918777 G ++
COPY TO SUKL REFINERY STANLOW MOV/0001 ++

REF SLW350047 30.08.89 1615

SUBJECT TRANMERE TO STANLOW BLACK OILS PIPELINE

WE REGRET TO INFORM YOU, UNDER THE CONDITIONS OF THE 'REPORTING
INJURIES, DISEASES AND DANGEROUS OCCURENCE REGULATIONS 1985', WE
HAVE HAD A FAILURE OF A 300 NS PIPELINE AT BROMBOROUGH IN WIRRAL
ON 19 AUGUST 1989.   THE PIPELINE, NO YP2140, RUNS FROM TRANMERE
TERMINAL TO EASTHAM TERMINAL, PARTLY IN PUBLIC LAND.   FROM EASTHAM
THE SERVICE IS CONTINUED AS LINE NO YP 1121 INTO STANLOW REFINERY
ENTIRELY IN PRIVATE LAND.

RESULTING FROM THIS FAILURE, APPROXIMATELY 150 CUBIC METRES OF
VENZUELAN CRUDE OIL WAS RELEASED ONTO A BEACH AND INTO THE RIVER
MERSEY AT ORDNANCE SURVEY GRID REFERENCE SJ 360832.   THE LEAK IS
NOW EFFECTIVELY SEALED AND THE LINE IS FILLED WITH SEAWATER.
ENVIRONMENTAL CLEAN UP IS PROCEEDING.   A FULL AND COMPREHENSIVE
REPORT OF THE INCIDENT IS IN COURSE OF PREPARATION AND WILL BE
FORWARDED TO YOU IN DUE COURSE.

+

NNNN✵
918777 energy g

APPENDIX L
NOTICE TO OWNERS REF. RIDDOR

NOTICE TO OWNERS

REPORTING OF INJURIES DISEASES

AND DANGEROUS OCCURRENCES REGULATIONS 1985

REPORTING OF PIPELINE INCIDENTS

By virtue of Regulation 3 of the Reporting of Injuries, Diseases and Dangerous Occurrences Regulations 1985 ("RIDDOR") the owners of pipelines as defined by section 65 of the Pipe-lines Act 1962 are required to notify the enforcing authority forthwith by the quickest practicable means of any occurrence of a kind specified in paragraph 12 of Part I of Schedule 1 to RIDDOR. They are also required to send a report to the enforcing authority on an approved form within 7 days. As explained in "A Guide to Riddor" issued in 1986 (HSE Reference HS(R)23), Sections 73 and 75, the enforcing authority in respect of 1962 Act pipe-lines is the Pipelines Inspectorate of the Safety Directorate at the Department of Energy, who act as Agents for HSE in matters concerning the safety of 1962 Act Pipe-lines.

Pipeline owners are therefore reminded that any notification or report required by RIDDOR in respect of an occurrence of a kind mentioned above should be made to the Pipelines Inspectorate in accordance with the Guidance. However, owners should note that the address and telephone number of the Pipelines Inspectorate given in Appendix 1 is now as follows:-

Telephone: 9 am to 5.30 pm on Working Days 01-238-3370

After hours and at weekends
- Duty Officer 01-276-5999

Address

The Pipelines Inspectorate
Safety Directorate
Petroleum Engineering Division
Department of Energy
1 Palace Street
London
SW1E 5HE

Telex No: 918777 ENERGYG

Fax No: 01 834 3771

Notification should be made immediately by telephone using the appropriate number mentioned above and the report (to follow within 7 days) should be on the approved form 2508 which appears in Appendix 2 of the Guidance.

D R CLEMENTSON
CHIEF PIPELINES INSPECTOR

APPENDIX M
PIPELINE INSPECTION HISTORY

INSPECTION AND METALLURGY

Ensuring Stanlow's
Integrity : Quality : Safety : Reliability

ENGINEERING INSPECTION SERVICES   26 AUGUST 1989

LINE No.   :   YP 2140   REPORT REF: EIS/2140/1

ROUTE   :   TRANMERE/EASTHAM (8" BRANCH TO U.M.L. POWER STATION)

LINE SIZE   :   300mm N.B. (SCH.30)

DESIGN TEMPERATURE :   80°C (UPRATED 1984 FROM 66°C)

DESIGN PRESSURE   :   40.0 BARS

COMMISSIONED :   CIRCA 1973

M.O.C.   :   API 5L GRADE B

INSPECTION HISTORY

DATE	COMMENTS
22.4.75	Bellows failed in service. Caused by inner sleeve fouling the expanding bellows section. New bellows unit fitted.
13.4.78	PAN 7508 : 200mm N.B. Line to U.M.L. Power Station fitted.
20.4.78	Beeches Yard. Sleeves shorting (C.P.) Lines excavated for C.P. repairs. (Opposite Royal Mersey Yacht Club).
26.3.79	Pressure Test. Satisfactory.
13.8.79	Leak reported at North Reclamation Site. Excavation, no leak found. Wrapping over was dislodged and was repaired using cold applied Bitumen wrapped tape.
16.4.80	Pressure Test. Satisfactory.
28.10.81	Pressure Test. Satisfactory.
9.10.82	Pressure Test. Satisfactory.
2.12.83	Pressure Test. Satisfactory.
JAN.1985	Design Temp. uprated from 66°C to 80°C : 4 new Incoloy 825 bellow units fitted.(Pit Nos: 12, 20, 27 & 28). The maximum working pressure was down-rated from 48 Bar.g to 40 Bar.g.
4.1.85	Pressure Test. Satisfactory.
OCT.1985	Cross connection to YP1121 installed in above ground pipetrack immediately outside the main gate of Shell's Eastham Installation.
7.2.86	Pressure Test. Satisfactory.

PIPELINE INSPECTION HISTORY

DATE	COMMENTS

15.1.87   Pressure Test. Satisfactory.

APR.1987   Line failed at North end of North Reclamation area on top of the
           embankment. The cause of failure was external corrosion. A Pearson
           survey was carried out along the North Reclamation embankment which
           highlighted wrapping breakdown in 4 other areas. Excavations
           revealed defective shrink wrapping at field joints. The shrink wraps
           and associated wrappings were removed and the pipe surface exposed.
           No corrosion was found. The field joints were made good, using cold
           applied bitumen wrap tape.

21.8.87   Action Report : North Reclamation. (Re-position anchor blocks
           opposite outfall). Action Report passed to Projects Department.

18.12.87   Diversion at Bromborough Dock. (As advised in our letter dated
           7 March 1988). The line was diverted from the shaft under the Lock
           gates, which have been replaced with an outfall/weir. The new
           section of line is embedded in sand/concrete casing forming part of
           the weir. This section is protected by an impressed current
           Cathodic Protection system.

4.2.88   Pressure Test. Satisfactory.

MAY 1989   Two valve connections installed in an above ground pipetrack
           immediately outside the boundary fence of Eastham Installation.

19.8.89   Line failed in service in Foreshore behind U.M.L. land between
           McIvors Slipway and Bromborough Power Station Jetty.

N.B.   All Pressure Testing carried out using Product over a 24 hour period,
       under a pressure generated by the pumps at Tranmere Installation.

       Cathodic Protection. Surveys are carried out at 6 monthly intervals.
       The last survey prior to the incident was carried out in March 1989.
       Records are available.

M364/AVG/MH

APPENDIX N
SCOPE OF WORK FOR CAPCIS

P.2

Department of Energy

Thames House South
Millbank London SW1P 4QJ
Telegrams Energy London SW1

Telephone Direct Line 01-238 2094
Switchboard 01-

	Your reference	
Dr C. Fowler		
CAPCIS- UMIST		
Bainbridge House	Our reference	Prep 4873
Granby Row		
Manchester M1 2PW	Date	23/8/1989

Dear Chris,

FAILURE INVESTIGATION OF CRACKED OIL PIPELINE

Further to our telephone discussions today please find
enclosed under cover of this letter a copy of an initial
scope of work in connection with the above problem.

We understand that you can provide personnel to attend
the field site tomorrow as agreed in the persons Dr F. A.
Golightly, Les Woolf & a photographer.

The Department would be pleased to receive your written
quotation for this work as soon as possible.

I envisage that the work would be done against a warrant
issued under the existing standing agreement between DEn
and CAPCIS.

Yours sincerely

F.I.Knight

Research & Development Branch

cc   D Southgate (PED 6)

MOST URGENT

SCOPE OF WORK FOR INVESTIGATION OF LEAK ON 12" SHELL OIL LINE
TRANMERE

PHASE I - SITE INVESTIGATION AND TRANSPORTATION

1.   Attend site and witness removal of damaged section from p:
and removal of temporary leak clamp.

2.   Close visual examination of damaged area plus video and st
photographs (colour).

3.   Take samples of river water, beach material, field-joint c
materials, factory-applied coating materials.

4.   Undertake CP survey if deemed necessary by D/Energy Inspec
D A Southgate).

5.   Undertake other such samples and surveys as may be agreed
D/Energy Inspector.

6.   Provide oral report to D/Energy Inspector without delay, :
by written report within 72 hours.

7.   Transport damaged pipe section in a secure manner to UMIS'
laboratories.

PHASE II - LABORATORY EXAMINATION & TESTS

1.   Full failure investigation including, but not limited to:

(a) Close examination of internal and external surfaces o
including radiographic inspection of weld areas.

(b) Full mechanical testing in accordance with BS 4515 a:
5L of parent metal, weld metal and HAZ area of pipe toget!
spectrographic analysis of same areas.

2.   Testing of wet beach material for pH and presence of othe:
injurious chemicals and/or presence of SRB organisms.

3.   Appropriate mechanical and chemical examination/tests of .
coating samples taken from site.

4.   Analysis of water samples for dissolved oxygen, pH, H_2S c
and SRB activity levels.

5.   Taking information from Phase II items 1-4 into account,
with full operational history of pipeline (to be supplied by S
produce recommendations on the probable mechanism(s) of failur

6.   Detailed report of test findings within target of 14 days
copies in draft, 10 of finalised version).

MOST URGENT

Notes

(i)   This investigation is to be treated as being "sub judice" until CAPCIS is informed by PED in writi[...] the contrary.

(ii)   Scope of work may be increased by D/Energy in th[...] of subsequent discussions with Shell management.

(iii)   Shell management may wish to appoint an employee observer.

(iv)   A copy of all Reports will be made available to [...] management by D/Energy.

(v)   Reports may also be made public.

(vi)   The investigation shall utilise Dr F Golightly and Mr L Woolf as principal investigators from UMIST/CAPCIS.

APPENDIX P
EXTRACTS FROM
CAPCIS REPORT
(13th MARCH 1990)

FIGURE 5   View of failure site looking north along the foreshore showing the concrete cover over the pipeline trench.

FIGURE 10   Pipe section removed from the pipeline (less the 30cm length removed from the north end—RHS in photograph above) in the as-received condition. The split in the pipe is arrowed.

(a)

(b)

FIGURE 14   Split in the pipe.

(Not to scale)

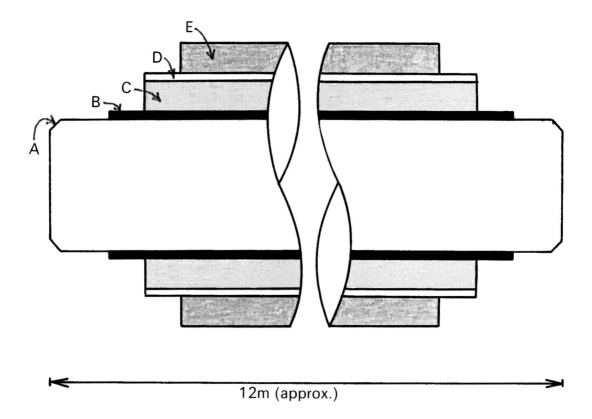

12m (approx.)

A—STEEL PIPE. 12 INCH DIA. × 0.33 INCH WALL THICKNESS
API 5L GRADE B MATERIAL

B—5mm (APPROX.) COAL TAR ENAMEL—CORROSION
PROTECTION

C—50mm (APPROX.) POLYURETHANE FOAM (PUF)—INSULATION

D—4mm (APPROX.) POLYPROPYLENE—MOULD FOR PUF

E—50mm (APPROX.) CONCRETE—WEIGHT COATING

FIGURE 49   Factory applied coatings.

(Not to scale)

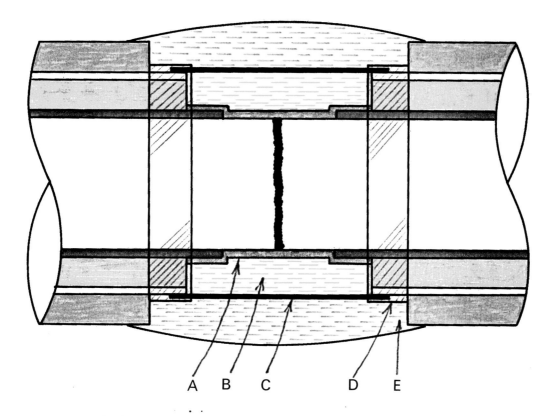

SEQUENCE OF SITE APPLIED MATERIALS:

A—POLYETHYLENE TAPE

B—POLYURETHANE FOAM

C—POLYETHYLENE HEAT SHRINK SLEEVE

D—POLYETHYLENE TAPE AT ENDS OF SLEEVE

E—CONCRETE

FIGURE 50   Completed field joint.

Printed in the United Kingdom for HMSO
Dd293761 C8 11/90